FOCUS ON FORMULA ONE

FORMULA ONE RACING CARS

BY HEATHER RULE

SportsZone
An Imprint of Abdo Publishing
abdobooks.com

abdobooks.com

Published by Abdo Publishing, a division of ABDO, PO Box 398166, Minneapolis, Minnesota 55439.

Printed in the United States of America, North Mankato, Minnesota.
052023
092023

THIS BOOK CONTAINS RECYCLED MATERIALS

Cover Photo: Bryn Lennon/Getty Images Sport/Getty Images
Interior Photos: Günther Molter/Klemantaski Collection/Hulton Archive/Getty Images, 4; Paul-Henri Cahier/Hulton Archive/Getty Images, 9 (left); Darren Heath/Hulton Archive/Getty Images, 9 (right); Miguel Schincariol/AFP/Getty Images, 10; Pascal Guyot/AFP/Getty Images, 11; Mark Thompson/Getty Images Sport/Getty Images, 12, 25; Shutterstock Images, 14–15; Urbanandsport/NurPhoto/Getty Images, 16, 28; Xavier Bonilla/NurPhoto/Getty Images, 19; Bryn Lennon/Getty Images Sport/Getty Images, 20; Tim Goode/PA Wire/AP Images, 22–23; Eric Cabanis/AFP/Getty Images, 27

Editor: Charlie Beattie
Series Designer: Michael J. Williams

Library of Congress Control Number: 2022949075

Publisher's Cataloging-in-Publication Data

Names: Rule, Heather, author.
Title: Formula one racing cars / by Heather Rule
Description: Minneapolis, Minnesota: Abdo Publishing Company, 2024 | Series: Focus on formula one | Includes online resources and index.
Identifiers: ISBN 9781098290757 (lib. bdg.) | ISBN 9781098276935 (ebook)
Subjects: LCSH: Formula One automobiles--Juvenile literature. | Racing cars--Juvenile literature. | Sports car racing--Juvenile literature.
Classification: DDC 796.72--dc23

TABLE OF

CONTENTS

Driver Juan Manuel Fangio races in an early front-engine car at the 1950 San Remo Grand Prix in Italy.

CHAPTER ONE

CAR BASICS AND CHANGES

Formula One racing cars are nothing like the cars people drive around town every day. Each Formula One car is made up of approximately 14,500 individual items. Though cars are designed following the same set of overall specifications, each one is unique. Teams fine-tune their cars, looking for any advantage that will help them on the track.

The cars have changed quite a bit since the first Formula One race in 1950. Everything from technology to safety is different. In the very first Grand Prix, the winning car topped out at

180 miles per hour (290 km/h). Cars today reach approximately 225 miles per hour (362 (km/h). One of the most noticeable changes is the location of the engine. For the sport's first five years, Formula One engines were in the front of the car. That caused one big problem. When a car would go into a corner, the weight would shift to the back wheels. With the heavy engine up front, the cars would understeer, meaning they would not turn well and go wide on the track. In 1955 the first rear-engine car appeared in Formula One. By 1961 all Formula One cars had rear engines.

THE ENGINES

Another major shift happened in 2014. That year the series shifted to hybrid technology to power its cars. Formula One had used V-8 engines. The new cars in 2014 were hybrids with

1.6-liter V-6 turbo engines. These engines have unique systems in them that recover both heat and kinetic energy. Recycling this waste energy gives each car approximately 160 brake horsepower for 33 seconds per lap on the track.

Changing from the V-8 to the turbocharged engines also created a new sound. The old engines were often compared to the sound of a swarm of wasps. The V-6 engines are still loud and impressive, but they have a much softer hum than the old machines.

HOW MUCH DOES IT COST?

Formula One limits how much money teams can spend. In 2022 teams had a $140 million budget for the season. That amount was set to drop to $135 million in 2023. Engines are the most expensive part of the car, estimated to cost approximately $10.5 million per year.

THE STEERING WHEEL

Even something as basic as the steering wheel has completely changed. At the start of Formula One, the steering wheel was made of aluminum and wood. Its only function was to steer the car. The modern steering wheel is made of carbon fiber, fiberglass, silicon, titanium, and copper. It's still used to steer the car. But as technology advanced, teams added more features to the wheel.

In the 2020s, steering wheels have roughly 20 interactive buttons and switches. Formula One drivers can use them to make changes to how the car runs on the track. For example, drivers can change their clutch and gear selection with paddle controls on the wheel. They can also change the car's brake balance or engine settings. One button automatically slows the car down in pit lane, where the speed limit drops to a certain limit,

On the left, a 1950s Formula One steering wheel. On the right, driver Fernando Alonso holds up a modern Formula One steering wheel.

depending on the specific track. Steering wheels are also custom built for each driver.

TIRES

Pirelli, a tire manufacturer, provides 18-inch (46-cm) tires for all Formula One cars. The series has seven different tire options to choose from throughout the season. Fans can identify the different tires by the strips of color on the outside.

Five tires, labeled C1 through C5, are slick and used for dry racetracks. C1 is the hardest rubber,

Formula One tires are stored inside custom blankets to keep them at an ideal temperature.

while C5 is the softest. Softer tires are considered faster. They also wear out sooner. Harder tires last longer, but they offer worse performance.

Race organizers inspect each track and choose which three slick tires to make available for that week's race. The slicks are color coded in white (hardest), yellow (middle), and red (softest). The most versatile slick tire, C3, is used at every Formula One race.

Two other options, labeled blue and green, are used on wet tracks. Green is the intermediate tire, and blue is the tire that will best grip the track in the wettest conditions.

Formula One regulations change and are updated each season. For decades Formula One cars had used 13-inch (33-cm) tires. One of the biggest changes in 2022 was to use 18-inch tires.

Lewis Hamilton's blue-striped rain tires helped him grip the wet track while cornering at the 2016 Monaco Grand Prix.

Max Verstappen won a Formula One record 15 races in 2022.

CHAPTER TWO

AERODYNAMICS

Max Verstappen won his second Formula One world championship in 2022. He won driving the Red Bull Racing RB18 car. The sharp-looking blue, red, and yellow car was one of the most successful cars in Formula One history.

New aerodynamics rules for Formula One cars in 2022 made car designs difficult for many teams. Red Bull's RB18 car was designed with distinctive sidepods that help with airflow to avoid drag. A car's sidepods contain radiators, but a team can change how the sidepods are constructed to reduce drag.

The more downforce a car is experiencing, the better it will stick to the track while cornering.

Formula One has a set of technical regulations for cars. But teams still have a lot of freedom to create their own advantages. Teams use computers to develop the car's parts and design. Top Formula One teams start this work more than

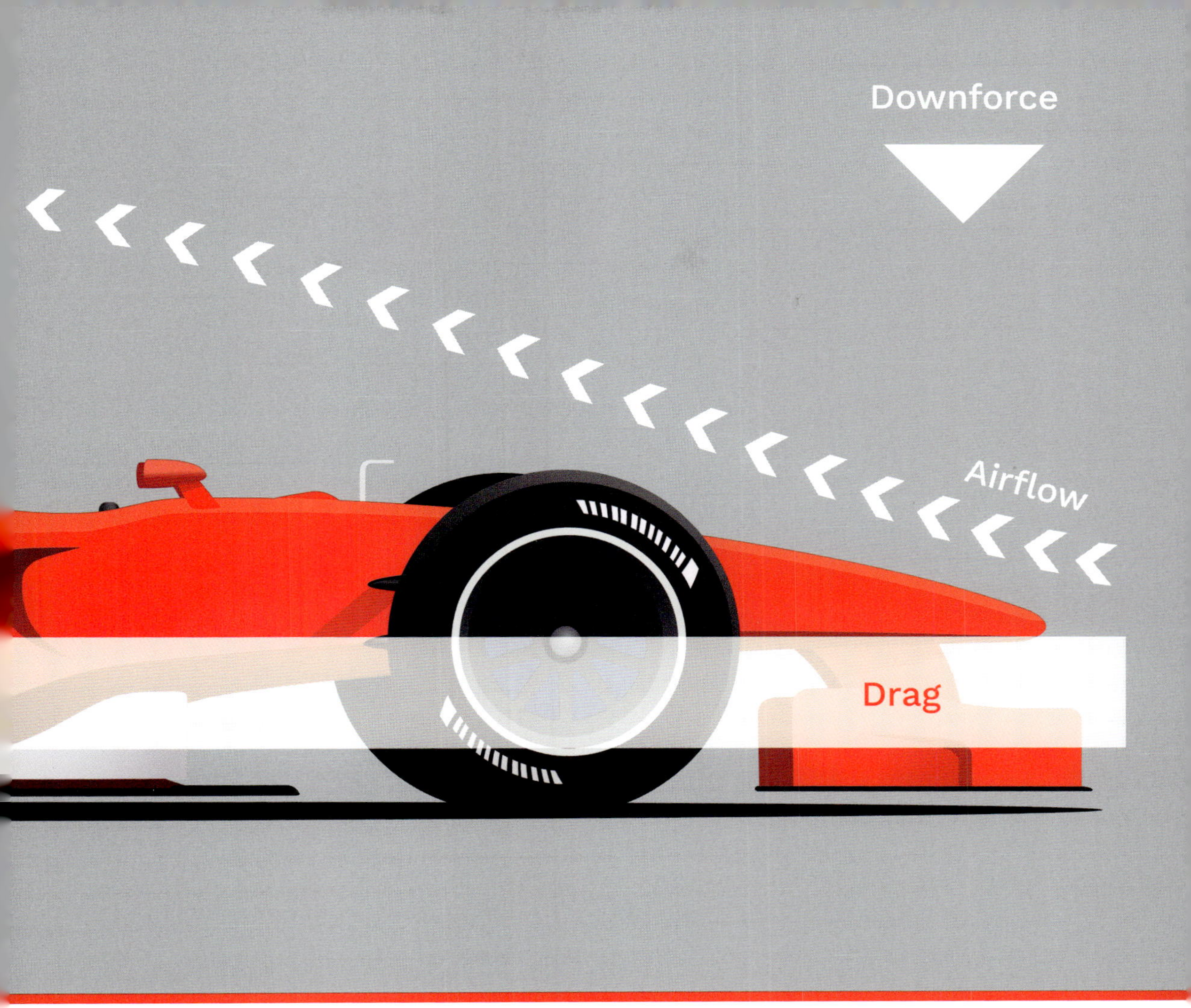

a season in advance of when the car will be on the track.

One main goal is to design a car that has the most efficient downforce. It is one of the most important parts of the car's design process.

An aerodynamic force is applied in a downward direction as the car moves forward on the track. Downforce improves a car's traction through corners.

SUSPENSION AND WINGS

A car's suspension is a big factor in aerodynamics. The suspension connects the car to its wheels. It is made up of springs, dampers, rockers,

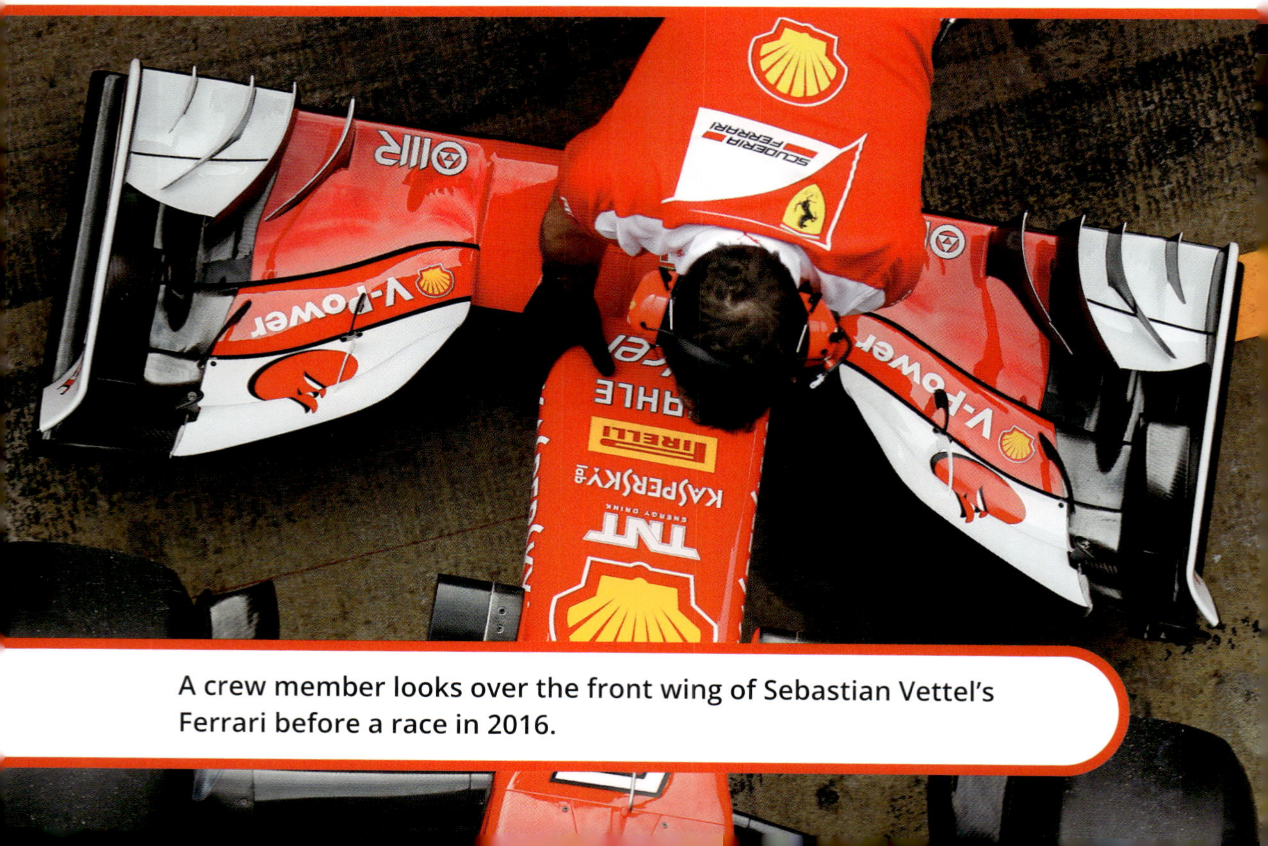

A crew member looks over the front wing of Sebastian Vettel's Ferrari before a race in 2016.

wishbones, axles, and pull and push rods. When teams choose to make changes to a car's setup for a race, those changes are usually made to the suspension. Suspension needs to be light enough not to weigh the car down. But it also has to be strong enough to hold the wheels to the car at high speeds while going over the corner curbs. Teams can set up the suspension to make sure tires and grip levels are the best combination for certain tracks.

CHANGING THE RULES

Technical rules for Formula One cars change each year. The changes implemented in 2022 led to many new design features on the cars. Formula One also restricted the freedom teams had to adjust their cars. The goal was to create closer competition among the teams.

Along with the suspension, teams can adjust the front and rear wings. The front wing is the first part of the car that encounters airflow. The wing needs to shift the airflow around the front tires to reduce drag. Having a good front wing will improve the overall performance of the car.

For rear wings, the drag-reduction system (DRS) was introduced in 2011. When the DRS is on, it allows part of the rear wing to open up when a driver is on a straightaway. The DRS lifts the leading edge of the wing up 2.8 inches (70 mm) to create a bigger gap. As a result, the car has less drag. The DRS closes automatically when the driver's foot lifts from the accelerator.

Lewis Hamilton's rear wing opens up as he attacks a straightaway.

Track crew members attempt to put out the fire after Romain Grosjean's crash at the 2020 Bahrain Grand Prix.

CHAPTER THREE

SAFETY

"And a big fire there!" Formula One fans heard the television announcer shout dramatically during the 2020 Bahrain Grand Prix. On their screens, an orange fireball and a large cloud of smoke filled the air outside Turn 3.

Driver Romain Grosjean's car had clipped another car and had crashed into a barrier. The car burst into flames as it broke in half. It was a scary sight, but Grosjean walked away from the crash with only minor burns on his hands. One major piece of the car saved his life—the Halo.

Driver Zhou Guanyu credited the Halo for saving his life during his frightening crash at the 2022 British Grand Prix.

The Halo first appeared on Formula One cars in 2018. The curved titanium bar is placed around

the top of the cockpit above the driver. Its main job is to protect a driver's head from large pieces of debris or from hitting the track if a car flips upside down. "I think it's the greatest thing we brought to Formula One," said Grosjean after his crash.

Head safety in motorsports has improved a lot over the years. Drivers started out wearing only goggles before switching to crash helmets. In 1996 a special headrest was introduced to help ease driver neck strain due to the strong g-forces while driving at high speeds.

HANS

The biggest support for a driver's head is the Head and Neck Support (HANS) device. These consist of pieces that strap to the back of the drivers' helmets. A HANS device limits how much a driver's head and neck can move around during a crash, which helps prevent serious injury.

A HANS device keeps a driver's head from whipping after a collision.

Formula One drivers have worn HANS devices since 2003. It wasn't popular at first. But it has been credited with saving drivers' lives.

The cars themselves are safer too. Creating the survival cell in the early 1980s was part of that. The cell, which is also known as the monocoque, is the tub where the cockpit is located. It's made of strong carbon fiber with layers of penetration-resistant Kevlar. These materials can absorb large amounts of energy in a crash. The cell is designed to be nearly indestructible. The idea is that it can survive even the worst crashes.

JACKIE STEWART CALLS FOR SAFETY

During his career in the late 1960s and early 1970s, three-time champion driver Jackie Stewart fought hard for better safety measures. The sport had seen 36 deaths between 1950 and 1973. Stewart fought to make seat belts mandatory, along with full-face helmets, track barriers, and safety teams.

LESSONS LEARNED

Crashes can result in direct safety changes.

Mika Häkkinen, *left*, collides with Johnny Herbert at the 1998 Belgian Grand Prix. The race helped change the way Formula One attaches tires to cars.

In the 1998 Belgian Grand Prix, a large crash sent several wheels flying off cars. Loose wheels can be dangerous to other cars, track workers, and even fans. To help prevent loose wheels from hitting others, cars were fitted with wheel tethers.

While Formula One will never be entirely without risk, the sport continues to develop new ways to improve safety.

They connect the wheels to the main body of the car, which is also known as the chassis.

Technology helps Formula One and its teams learn from crashes. Accident-data recorders are in all Formula One cars. These recorders capture information about what happens in a crash. Analyzing this data can help the series improve driver safety. Driver-facing cameras in the cockpit work with these recorders to provide additional views and data. It's not possible to make Formula One racing 100 percent risk-free. But the series has come a long way over the years to make cars safer.

GLOSSARY

aerodynamics
The study of moving air around a solid object.

brake balance
The distribution of brake force applied to the front and rear wheels of a Formula One car.

brake horsepower
The amount of power generated by an engine working under ideal conditions.

chassis
The main part of the car, where the engine and suspension are attached.

drag
Air resistance a car experiences as it travels forward on the track.

g-force
A physical force equal to one unit of gravity that can be multiplied by fast changes of direction.

grand prix
From the French for "grand prize," any race that is part of the Formula One championship series.

regulations
Rules.

suspension
A system that connects all four wheels of the car and absorbs shock from the road while driving.

traction
Friction that causes a moving object to stick to a surface.

MORE INFORMATION

BOOKS

Hewson, Anthony K. *Formula One Grand Prix Races*. Minneapolis, MN: Abdo Publishing, 2024.

Hustad, Douglas. *Innovations in Auto Racing*. Minneapolis, MN: Abdo Publishing, 2022.

Rule, Heather. *GOATs of Auto Racing*. Minneapolis, MN: Abdo Publishing, 2022.

ONLINE RESOURCES

Booklinks
NONFICTION NETWORK
FREE! ONLINE NONFICTION RESOURCES

To learn more about Formula One cars, please visit **abdobooklinks.com** or scan this QR code. These links are routinely monitored and updated to provide the most current information available.

INDEX

ABOUT THE AUTHOR

Heather Rule is a freelance sports journalist, author, and social media coordinator. She has a bachelor's degree in journalism and mass communication from the University of St. Thomas in St. Paul, Minnesota.